HAL•LEONARD

JAZZ PLAY-ALONG®

Book & Audio for B♭, E♭, C and Bass Clef Instruments

Latin J
10 Latin Jazz Classics

volume 23

Arranged and Produced
by Mark Taylor

	C Treble Instruments	B♭ Instruments	E♭ Instruments	C Bass Instruments
AGUA DE BEBER (WATER TO DRINK)	4	24	44	64
INVITATION	6	26	46	66
CHEGA DE SAUDADE (NO MORE LIES)	8	28	48	68
WATCH WHAT HAPPENS	10	30	50	70
SWEET HAPPY LIFE (SAMBA DE ORPHEO)	12	32	52	72
THE GIFT! (RECADO BOSSA NOVA)	14	34	54	74
MAS QUE NADA	16	36	56	76
MANHA DE CARNIVAL (A DAY IN THE LIFE OF A FOOL)	18	38	58	78
SO NICE (SUMMER SAMBA)	20	40	60	80
RAN KAN KAN	22	42	62	82
LYRICS				84

PLAYBACK+
Speed • Pitch • Balance • Loop

To access audio, visit:
www.halleonard.com/mylibrary

3892-8276-1641-3265

ISBN 978-0-634-06713-6

HAL•LEONARD®

Visit Hal Leonard Online at
www.halleonard.com

World headquarters, contact:
Hal Leonard
7777 West Bluemound Road
Milwaukee, WI 53213
Email: info@halleonard.com

In Europe, contact:
Hal Leonard Europe Limited
1 Red Place
London, W1K 6PL
Email: info@halleonardeurope.com

In Australia, contact:
Hal Leonard Australia Pty. Ltd.
4 Lentara Court
Cheltenham, Victoria, 3192 Australia
Email: info@halleonard.com.au

LATIN JAZZ

Volume 23

Arranged and Produced by
Mark Taylor & Jim Roberts

Featured Players:

Graham Breedlove-Trumpet
John Desalme-Alto Sax
Tony Nalker-Piano
Jim Roberts-Bass & Guitar
Steve Fidyk-Drums

Recorded at Bias Studios, Springfield, Virginia
Bob Dawson, Engineer

HOW TO USE THE AUDIO:

Each song has <u>two</u> tracks:

1) Split Track/Demonstration

Woodwind, Brass, Keyboard, and **Mallet Players** can use this track as a learning tool for melody, style and inflection.

Bass Players can learn and perform with this track – remove the recorded bass track by turning down the volume on the LEFT channel.

Keyboard and **Guitar Players** can learn and perform with this track – remove the recorded piano part by turning down the volume on the RIGHT channel.

2) Backing Track

Soloists or **Groups** can learn and perform with this accompaniment track with the RHYTHM SECTION only.

AGUA DE BEBER
(WATER TO DRINK)

ENGLISH WORDS BY NORMAN GIMBEL
PORTUGUESE WORDS BY VINICIUS DE MORAES
MUSIC BY ANTONIO CARLOS JOBIM

C VERSION

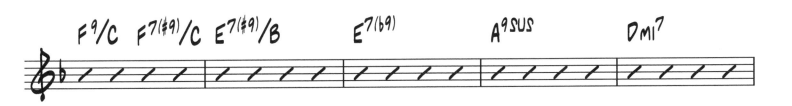

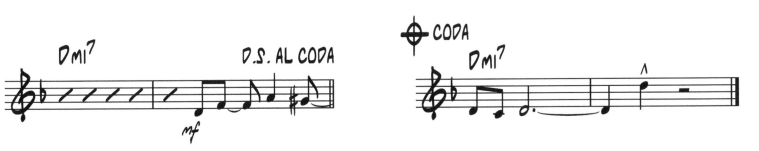

INVITATION

WORDS BY PAUL FRANCIS WEBSTER
MUSIC BY BRONISLAU KAPER

CHEGA DE SAUDADE
(NO MORE BLUES)

ENGLISH LYRIC BY
JON HENDRICKS AND JESSIE CAVANAUGH
ORIGINAL TEXT BY VINICIUS DE MORAES
MUSIC BY ANTONIO CARLOS JOBIM

C VERSION

WATCH WHAT HAPPENS

MUSIC BY MICHEL LEGRAND
ORIGINAL FRENCH TEXT BY JACQUES DEMY
ENGLISH LYRICS BY NORMAN GIMBEL

C VERSION

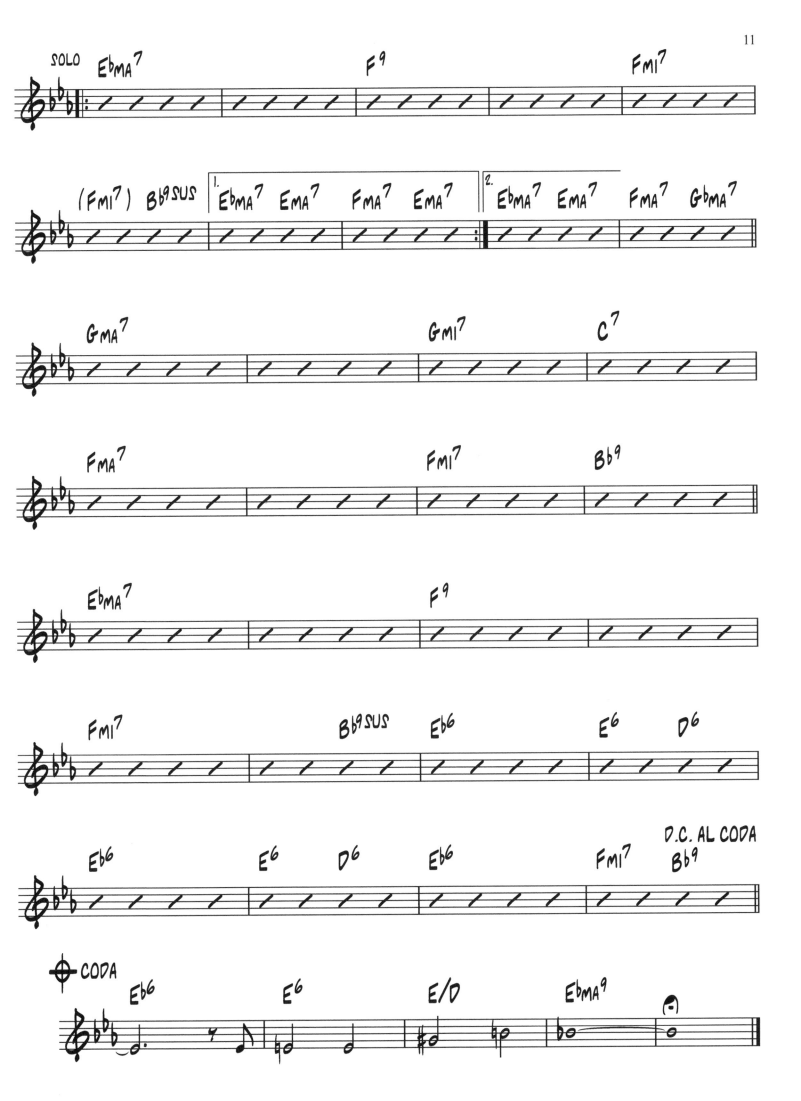

SWEET HAPPY LIFE
(SAMBA DE ORPHEO)

ENGLISH WORDS BY NORMAN GIMBEL
ORIGINAL PROTUGUESE WORDS BY ANTONIO MARIA
MUSIC BY LUIZ BONFA

C VERSION

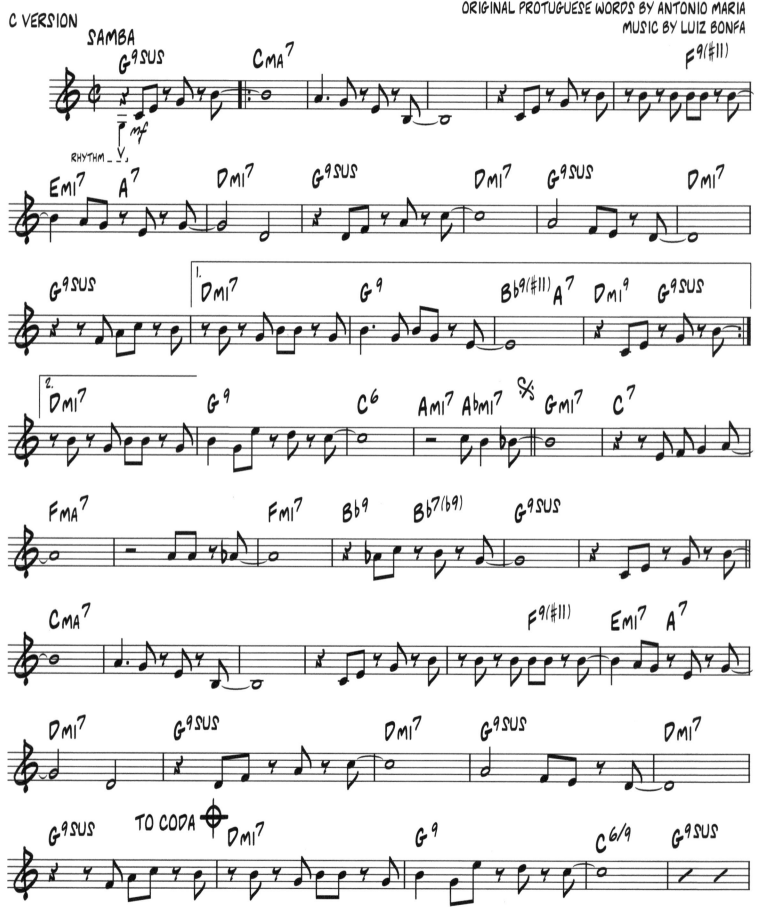

THE GIFT!
(RECADO BOSSA NOVA)

MUSIC BY DJALMA FERREIRA
ORIGINAL LYRIC BY LUIZ ANTONIO
ENGLISH LYRIC BY PAUL FRANCIS WEBSTER

C VERSION

MAS QUE NADA

WORDS AND MUSIC BY
JORGE BEN

C VERSION

MANHA DE CARNAVAL
(A DAY IN THE LIFE OF A FOOL)

WORDS BY CARL SIGMAN
MUSIC BY LUIZ BONFA

C VERSION

SO NICE
(SUMMER SAMBA)

ORIGINAL WORDS AND MUSIC BY
MARCOS VALLE AND PAULO SERGIO VALLE
ENGLISH WORDS BY NORMAN GIMBEL

C VERSION

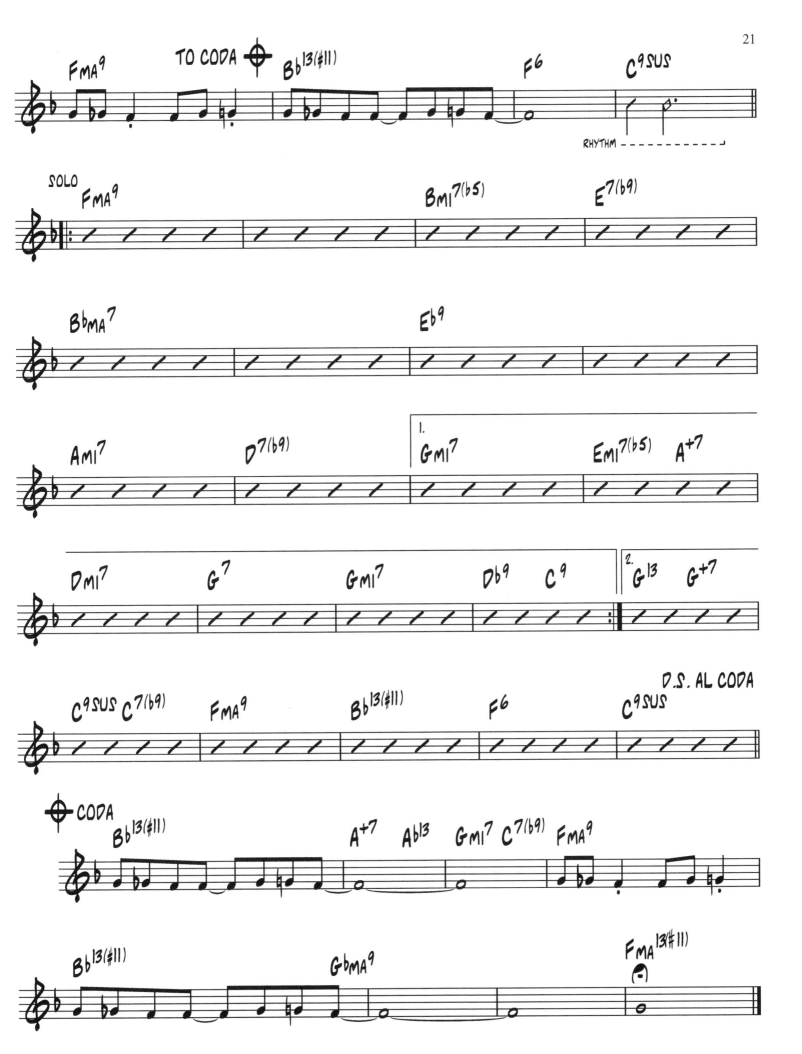

RAN KAN KAN

C VERSION

MUSIC BY TITO PUENTE

AGUA DE BEBER
(WATER TO DRINK)

ENGLISH WORDS BY NORMAN GIMBEL
PORTUGUESE WORDS BY VINICIUS DE MORAES
MUSIC BY ANTONIO CARLOS JOBIM

B♭ Version

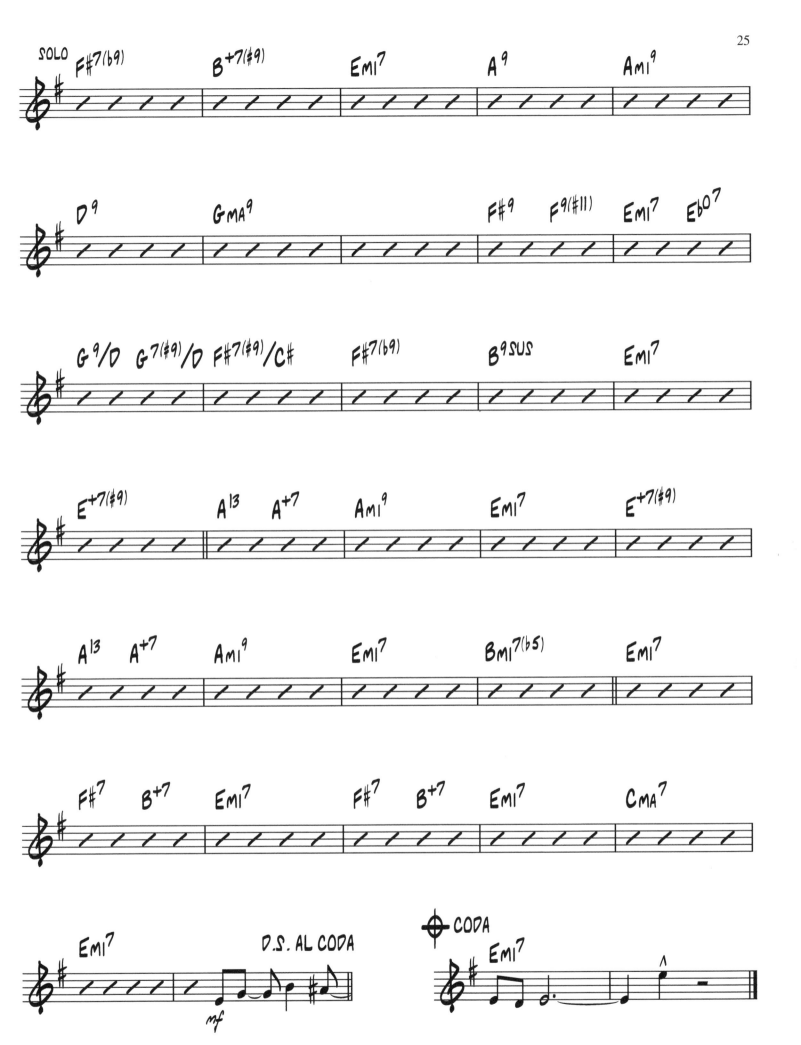

INVITATION

WORDS BY PAUL FRANCIS WEBSTER
MUSIC BY BRONISLAU KAPER

CHEGA DE SAUDADE
(NO MORE BLUES)

ENGLISH LYRIC BY
JON HENDRICKS AND JESSIE CAVANAUGH
ORIGINAL TEXT BY VINICIUS DE MORAES
MUSIC BY ANTONIO CARLOS JOBIM

Bb VERSION

MEDIUM BOSSA

Watch What Happens

MUSIC BY MICHEL LEGRAND
ORIGINAL FRENCH TEXT BY JACQUES DEMY
ENGLISH LYRICS BY NORMAN GIMBEL

Bb VERSION

SWEET HAPPY LIFE
(SAMBA DE ORPHEO)

ENGLISH WORDS BY NORMAN GIMBEL
ORIGINAL PROTUGUESE WORDS BY ANTONIO MARIA
MUSIC BY LUIZ BONFA

Bb Version

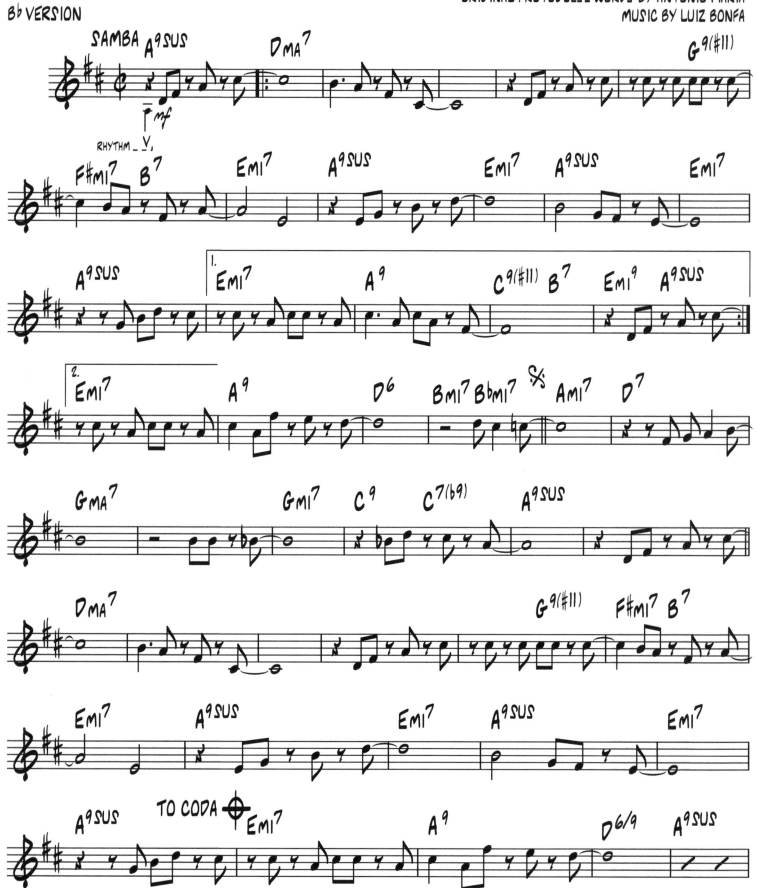

THE GIFT!
(RECADO BOSSA NOVA)

MUSIC BY DJALMA FERREIRA
ORIGINAL LYRIC BY LUIZ ANTONIO
ENGLISH LYRIC BY PAUL FRANCIS WEBSTER

Bb Version

Mas Que Nada

WORDS AND MUSIC BY
JORGE BEN

Bb VERSION

MANHA DE CARNAVAL
(A DAY IN THE LIFE OF A FOOL)

WORDS BY CARL SIGMAN
MUSIC BY LUIZ BONFA

39

SO NICE
(SUMMER SAMBA)

ORIGINAL WORDS AND MUSIC BY
MARCOS VALLE AND PAULO SERGIO VALLE
ENGLISH WORDS BY NORMAN GIMBEL

Bb Version

41

Ran Kan Kan

Bb VERSION

MUSIC BY TITO PUENTE

Agua de Beber
(WATER TO DRINK)

ENGLISH WORDS BY NORMAN GIMBEL
PORTUGUESE WORDS BY VINICIUS DE MORAES
MUSIC BY ANTONIO CARLOS JOBIM

Eb Version

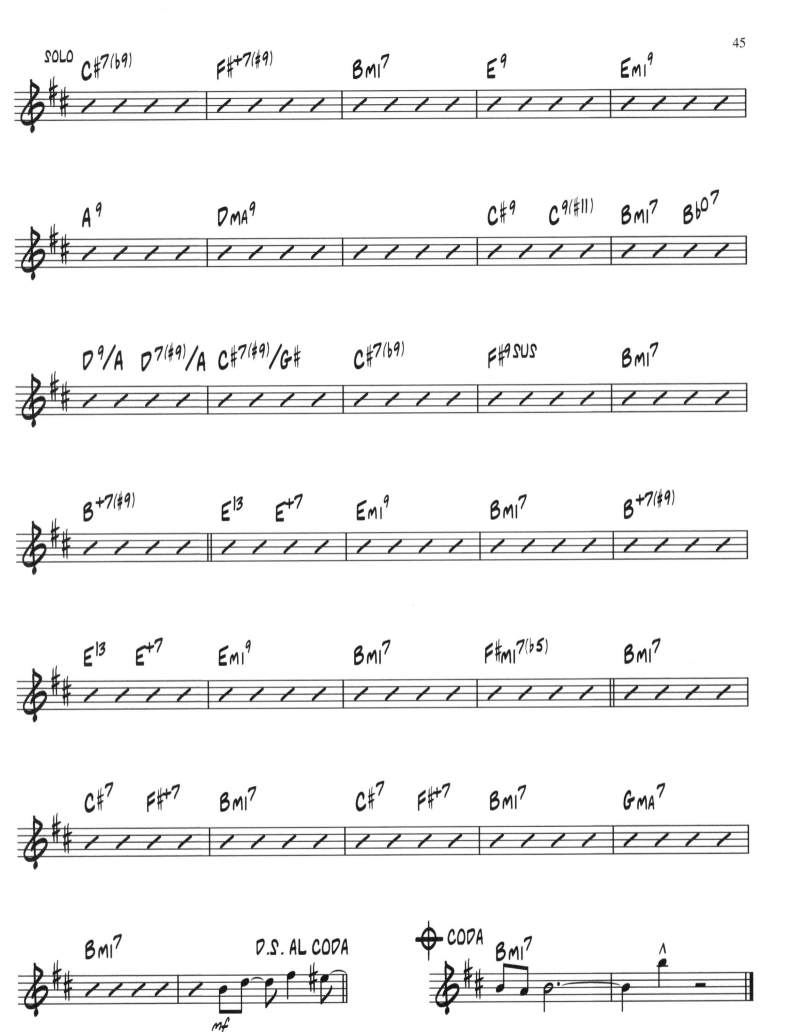

INVITATION

WORDS BY PAUL FRANCIS WEBSTER
MUSIC BY BRONISLAU KAPER

47

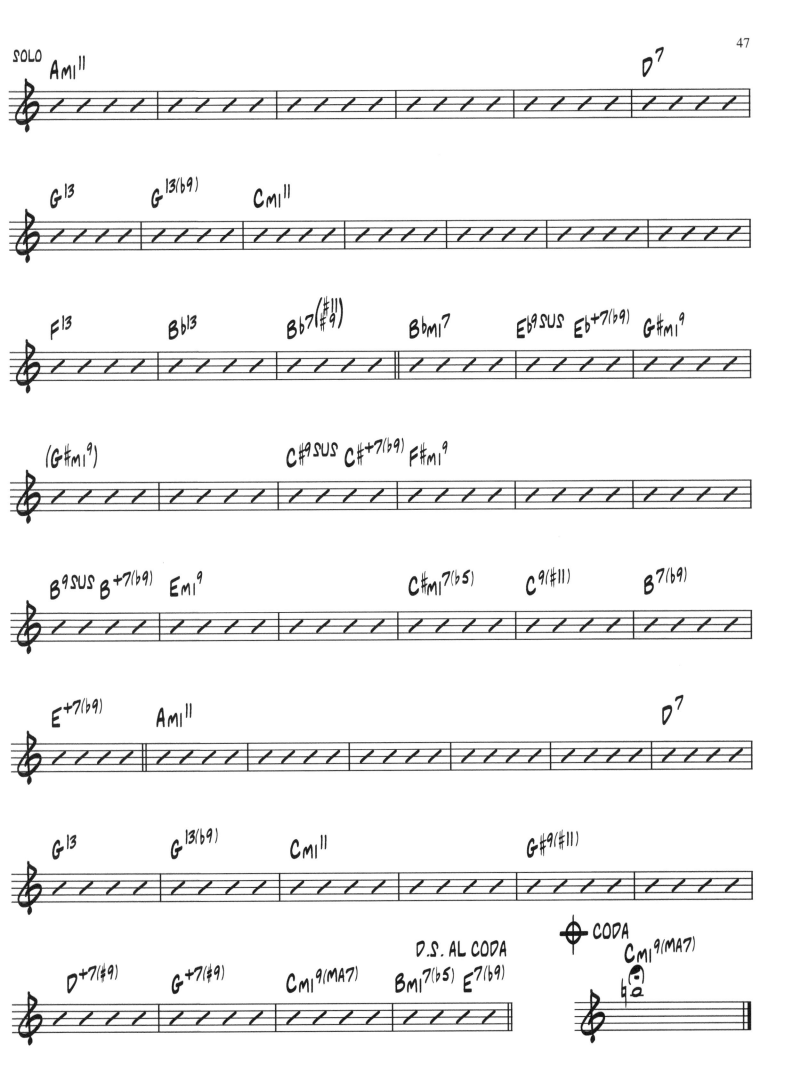

CHEGA DE SAUDADE
(NO MORE BLUES)

ENGLISH LYRIC BY
JON HENDRICKS AND JESSIE CAVANAUGH
ORIGINAL TEXT BY VINICIUS DE MORAES
MUSIC BY ANTONIO CARLOS JOBIM

Eb VERSION

MEDIUM BOSSA

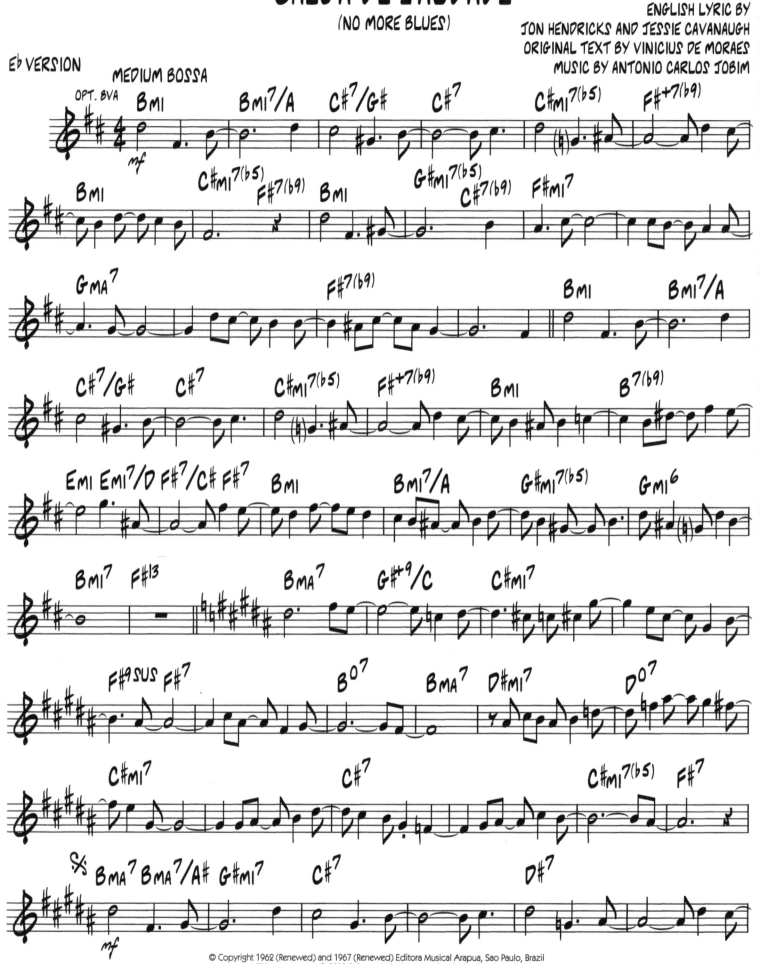

WATCH WHAT HAPPENS

MUSIC BY MICHEL LEGRAND
ORIGINAL FRENCH TEXT BY JACQUES DEMY
ENGLISH LYRICS BY NORMAN GIMBEL

Eb VERSION

MEDIUM LATIN

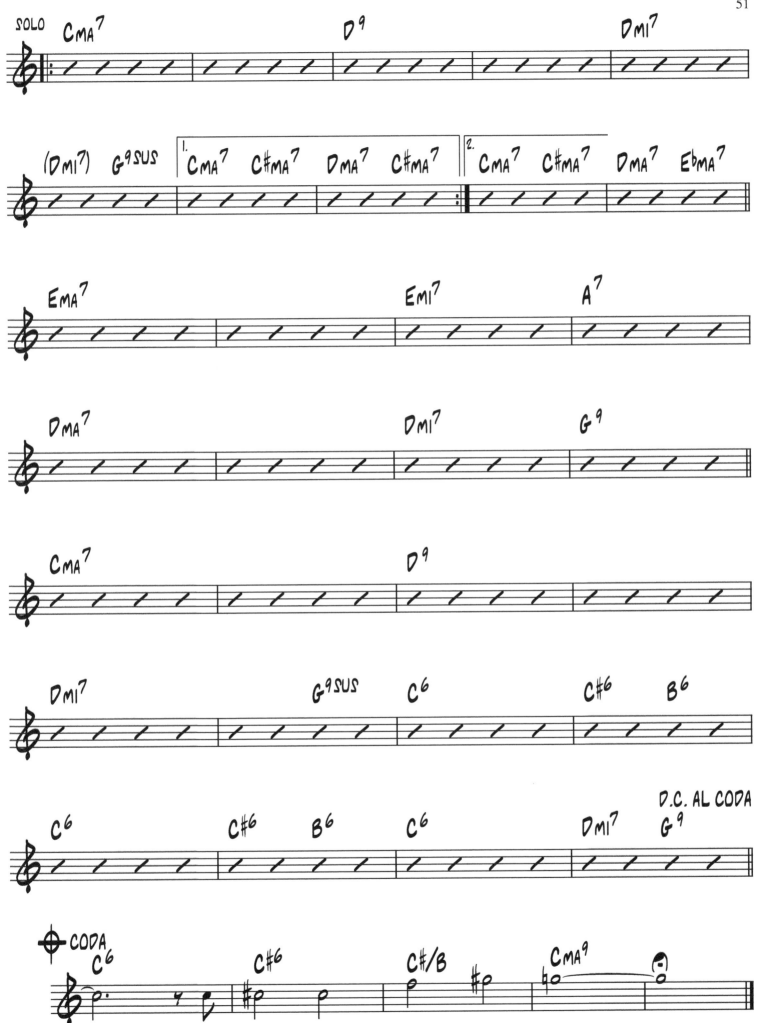

SWEET HAPPY LIFE
(SAMBA DE ORPHEO)

ENGLISH WORDS BY NORMAN GIMBEL
ORIGINAL PROTUGUESE WORDS BY ANTONIO MARIA
MUSIC BY LUIZ BONFA

Eb VERSION

THE GIFT!
(RECADO BOSSA NOVA)

MUSIC BY DJALMA FERREIRA
ORIGINAL LYRIC BY LUIZ ANTONIO
ENGLISH LYRIC BY PAUL FRANCIS WEBSTER

Eb VERSION

55

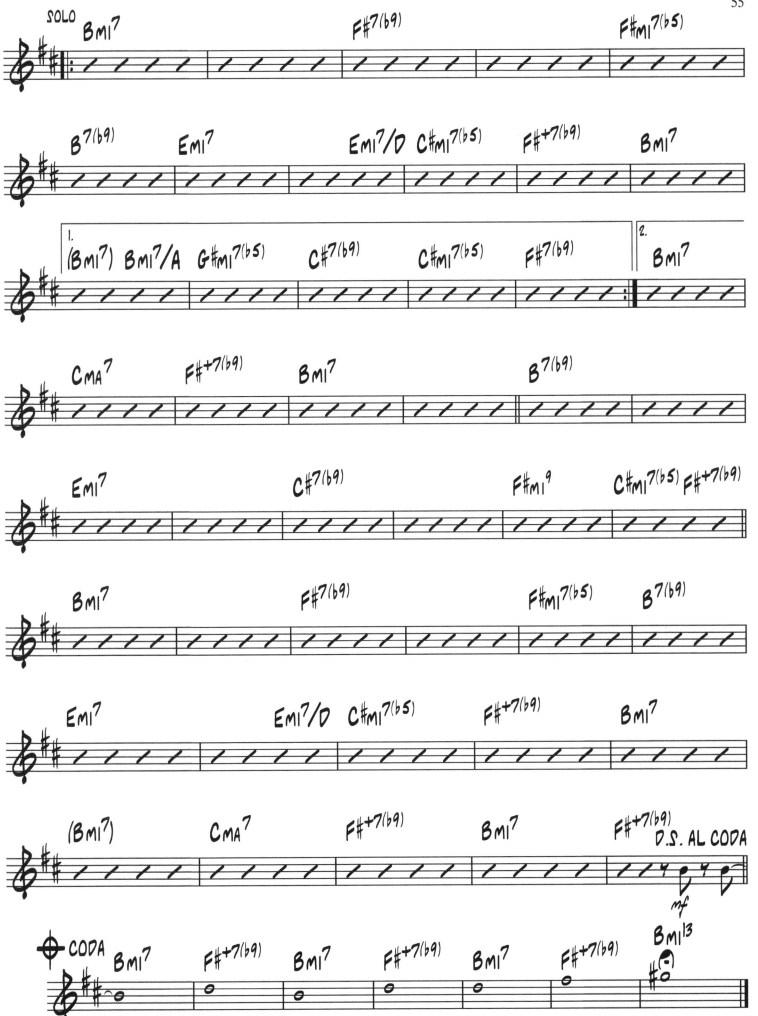

MAS QUE NADA

WORDS AND MUSIC BY
JORGE BEN

MANHA DE CARNAVAL
(A DAY IN THE LIFE OF A FOOL)

WORDS BY CARL SIGMAN
MUSIC BY LUIZ BONFA

SO NICE
(SUMMER SAMBA)

ORIGINAL WORDS AND MUSIC BY
MARCOS VALLE AND PAULO SERGIO VALLE
ENGLISH WORDS BY NORMAN GIMBEL

61

RAN KAN KAN

E♭ VERSION

MUSIC BY TITO PUENTE

AGUA DE BEBER
(WATER TO DRINK)

ENGLISH WORDS BY NORMAN GIMBEL
PORTUGUESE WORDS BY VINICIUS DE MORAES
MUSIC BY ANTONIO CARLOS JOBIM

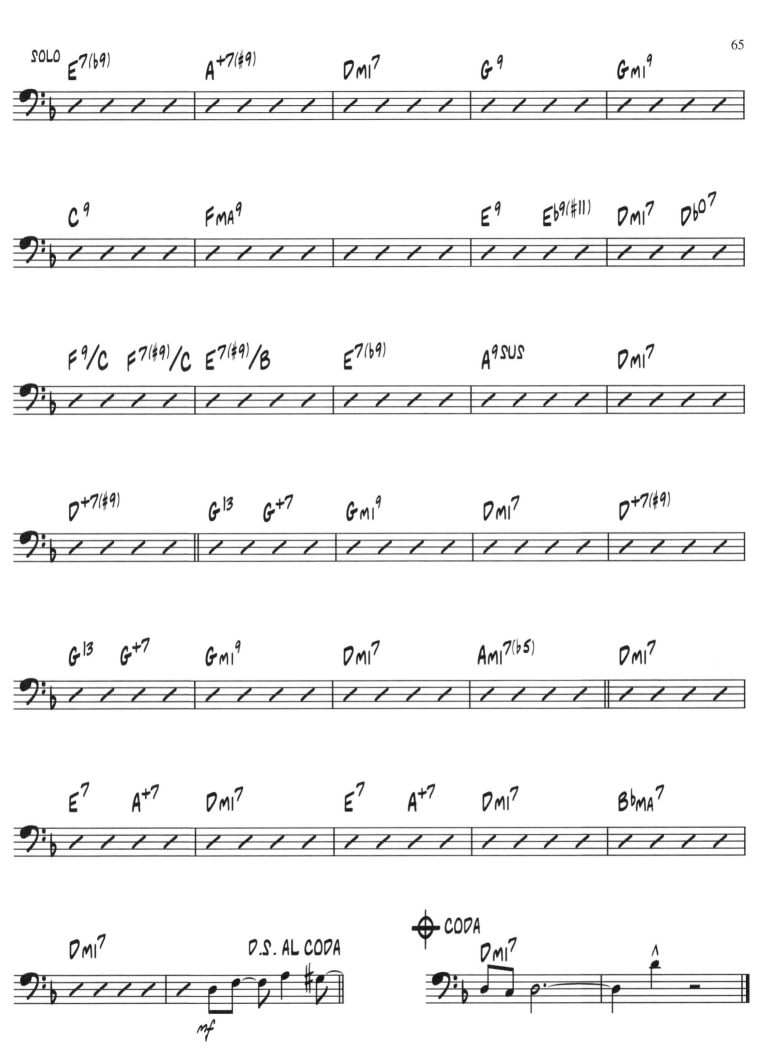

INVITATION

WORDS BY PAUL FRANCIS WEBSTER
MUSIC BY BRONISLAU KAPER

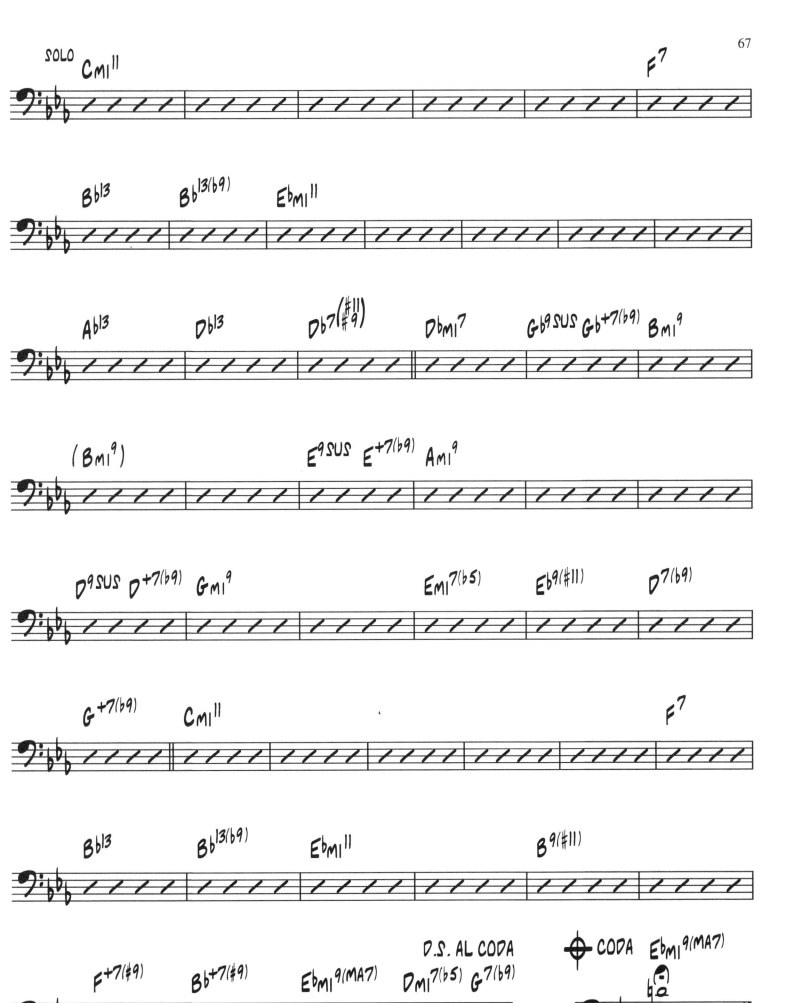

CHEGA DE SAUDADE
(NO MORE BLUES)

ENGLISH LYRIC BY
JON HENDRICKS AND JESSIE CAVANAUGH
ORIGINAL TEXT BY VINICIUS DE MORAES
MUSIC BY ANTONIO CARLOS JOBIM

Watch What Happens

MUSIC BY MICHEL LEGRAND
ORIGINAL FRENCH TEXT BY JACQUES DEMY
ENGLISH LYRICS BY NORMAN GIMBEL

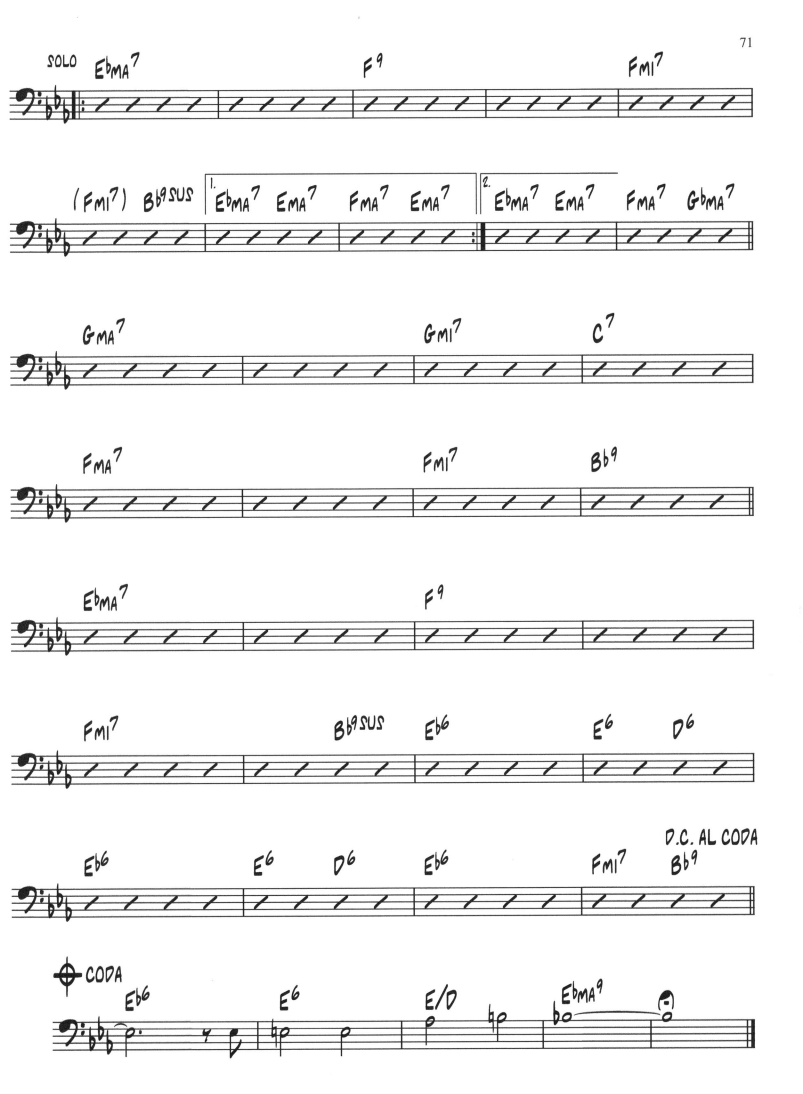

SWEET HAPPY LIFE
(SAMBA DE ORPHEO)

English Words by Norman Gimbel
Original Protuguese Words by Antonio Maria
Music by Luiz Bonfa

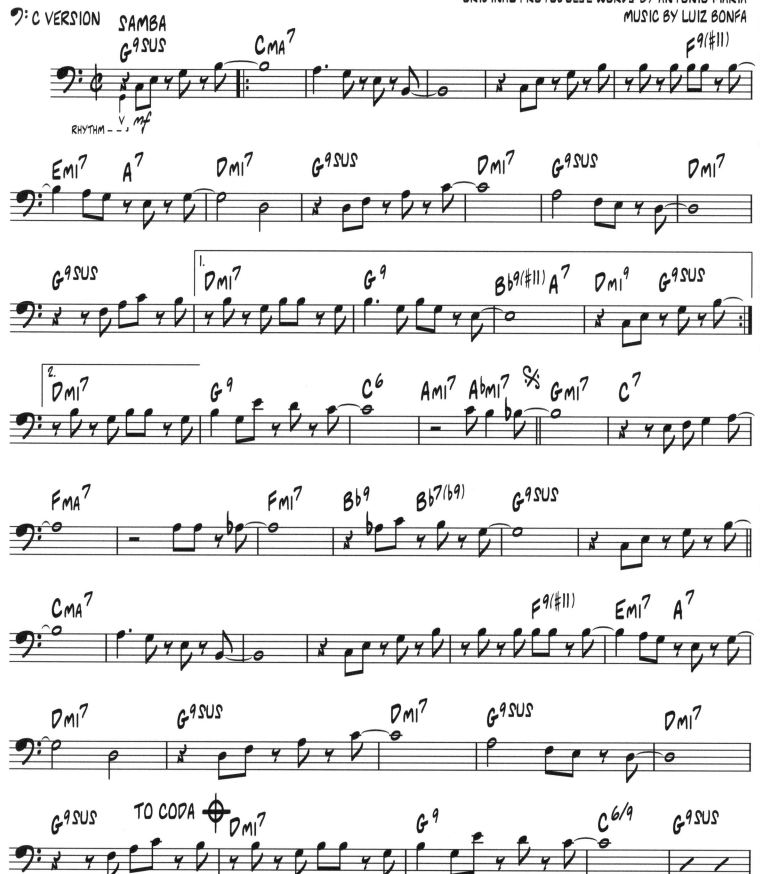

THE GIFT!
(RECADO BOSSA NOVA)

MUSIC BY DJALMA FERREIRA
ORIGINAL LYRIC BY LUIZ ANTONIO
ENGLISH LYRIC BY PAUL FRANCIS WEBSTER

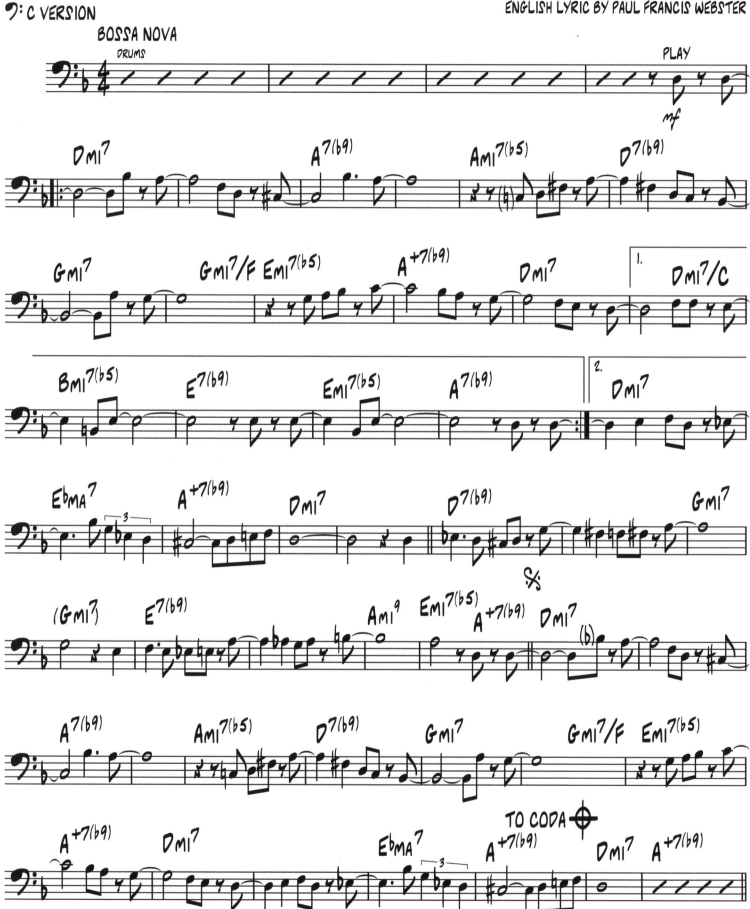

Mas Que Nada

WORDS AND MUSIC BY
JORGE BEN

MANHA DE CARNAVAL
(A DAY IN THE LIFE OF A FOOL)

WORDS BY CARL SIGMAN
MUSIC BY LUIZ BONFA

SO NICE
(SUMMER SAMBA)

ORIGINAL WORDS AND MUSIC BY
MARCOS VALLE AND PAULO SERGIO VALLE
ENGLISH WORDS BY NORMAN GIMBEL

𝄢 C VERSION

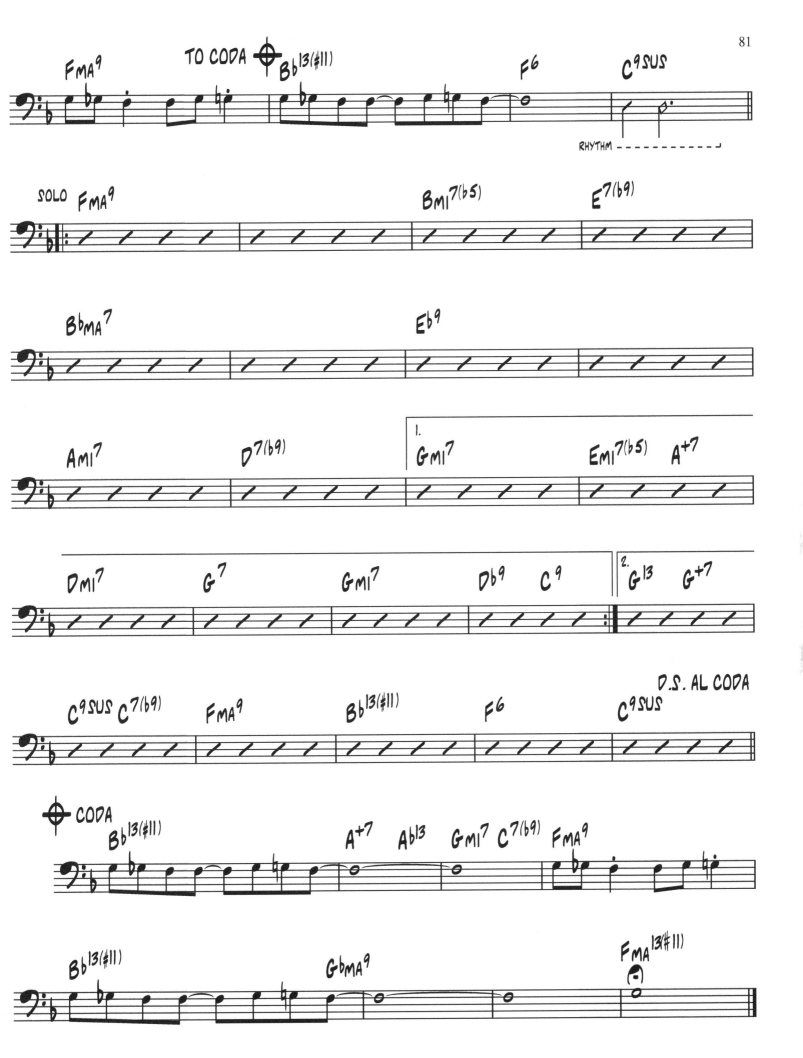

RAN KAN KAN

MUSIC BY TITO PUENTE

Lyrics
(English Only)

AGUA DE BEBER
(Water To Drink)

Your love is rain, my heart the flower.
I need your love or I will die.
My very life is in your power.
Will I wither and fade or bloom to the sky?
Agua De Beber,
Give the flower water to drink.
Agua De Beber,
Give the flower water to drink.

The rain can fall on distant deserts.
The rain can fall upon the sea.
The rain can fall upon the flower.
Since the rain has to fall let it fall on me.
Agua De Beber, Agua De Beber camara,
Agua De Beber, Agua De Beber camara.

INVITATION

You and your smile
Hold a strange Invitation.
Somehow it seems
We've shared our dreams, But where?
Time after time in a room full of strangers,
Out of the blue suddenly you are there.
Wherever I go
You're the glow of temptation,
Glancing my way in the gray of the dawn.

And always your eyes
Smile that strange Invitation.
Then you are gone,
Where, oh, where have you gone?
How long must I stay in a world of illusion,
Be where you are, so near yet so far apart.
Hoping you'll say with a warm Invitation,
"Where have you been?
Darling come into my heart."

CHEGA DE SAUDADE
(No More Blues)

No more blues,
I'm goin' back home.
No, no more blues,
I promise no more to roam.
Home is where the heart is,
The funny part is
My heart's been right there all along.
No more tears and no more sighs,
And no more fears,
I'll say no more goodbyes.
If travel beckons me
I swear I'm gonna refuse,
I'm gonna settle down
And there'll be no more blues.

Every day while I am far away
My thoughts turn homeward,
Forever homeward.
I traveled 'round the world
In search of happiness,
But all the happiness I found
Was in my hometown.
No more blues, I'm goin' back home.
No, no more dues,
I'm through with all my wandrin', now
I'll settle down and live my life
And build a home with no more strife,
When we settle down,
There'll be no more blues,
Nothin' but happiness.
When we settle down
There'll be no more blues.

WATCH WHAT HAPPENS

Let someone start believing in you.
Let him hold out his hand.
Let him touch you and
Watch what happens.
One someone who can look in your eyes
And see into your heart,
Let him find you and watch what Happens.

Cold, no I won't believe your heart is cold
Maybe just afraid to be broken again.
Let someone with a deep love to give,
Give that deep love to you
And what magic you'll see:
Let someone give his heart,
Someone who cares like me.

SWEET HAPPY LIFE
(Samba De Orfeo)

My wish for you: sweet happy life.
May all the days of the years that you live
Be laughing days.
With all my heart: sweet happy life.
And may the night times that follow the days
Be dancing nights. (Repeat once to beginning)
Stars for your smile,
Moons for your hair,
And someone's wonderful love
For your loving heart to share.
My wish for you: sweet happy life.
May all your sorrows be gone and your heart
Begin to sing.
And if a wish can make it be,
I wish you spend ev'ry day
Of your happy life with me.
Sweet happy life, Sweet happy life.

THE GIFT!
(Recado Bossa Nova)

No string of pearls in a velvet glove,
The gift I bring you is the gift of love.
No ring of gold but a dream to enfold,
When all the stars have flown
And we're alone.

The gift of love is a precious thing,
A touch of magic on a day in spring.
The golden dream ev'ry dreamer pursues
Remember darling,
Never refuse the gift of love.

For love can be a melody that lingers,
Or slip like April wine
Right thru your fingers.

So kiss me sweet
Till our secret star
Illuminates the way to Shangri-La!
Whatever fate may befall all I know
Is that the gift of love is
The greatest gift of all.
The gift of love is the greatest gift of all.

MAS QUE NADA

Ooo, when your eyes meet mine. Pow! Pow! Pow!
Ooo, I could lose my mind. Ow! Ow! Ow!
It's a feeling that begins to grow an' grow an' grow inside me,
'Til I feel like I'm gonna explode.
Oh, this is what you do to me.
Are your lips saying things that you feel in your heart?
If your heart is beating madly, then let the music start.
Hold me, hold me!
It's heaven, oo, it's heaven when you hold me!
I want you night and day.
Ooo, I want you here to stay.
Ooo, when your eyes meet mine.
Pow! Pow! Pow! Ooo, I could lose my mind.

MANHA DE CARNAVAL
(A Day In The Life Of A Fool)

A Day In The Life Of A Fool,
A sad and a long, lonely day,
I walk the avenue and hope I'll run into
The welcome sight of you coming my way.
I stop just across from your door
But you're never home anymore.
So back to my room and there in the gloom
I cry tears of goodbye.
'Til you come back to me,
That's the way it will be
Ev'ry day in the life of a fool.

SO NICE
(Summer Samba)

Someone to hold me tight, that would be very nice,
Someone to love me right, that would be very nice.
Someone to understand each little dream in me,
Someone to take my hand, to be a team with me.
So Nice, life would be so nice if one day
I'd find someone who would take my hand
And samba through life with me.
Someone to cling to me,
Stay with me right or wrong,
Someone to sing to me
Some little samba song.
Someone to take my heart, then give his heart to me.
Someone who's ready to give love a start with me.
Oh yes, that would be so nice.
Should it be you and me, I could see it would be nice.
Ooo, I want you here to stay.

The Best-Selling Jazz Book of All Time Is Now Legal!

The Real Books are the most popular jazz books of all time. Since the 1970s, musicians have trusted these volumes to get them through every gig, night after night. The problem is that the books were illegally produced and distributed, without any regard to copyright law, or royalties paid to the composers who created these musical masterpieces.

Hal Leonard is very proud to present the first legitimate and legal editions of these books ever produced. You won't even notice the difference, other than all the notorious errors being fixed: the covers and typeface look the same, the song lists are nearly identical, and the price for our edition is even cheaper than the originals!

Every conscientious musician will appreciate that these books are now produced accurately and ethically, benefitting the songwriters that we owe for some of the greatest tunes of all time!

VOLUME 1
00240221	C Edition	$49.99
00240224	B♭ Edition	$49.99
00240225	E♭ Edition	$49.99
00240226	Bass Clef Edition	$49.99
00286389	F Edition	$39.99
00240292	C Edition 6 x 9	$39.99
00240339	B♭ Edition 6 x 9	$44.99
00147792	Bass Clef Edition 6 x 9	$39.99
00200984	Online Backing Tracks: Selections	$45.00
00110604	Book/USB Flash Drive Backing Tracks Pack	$85.00
00110599	USB Flash Drive Only	$50.00

VOLUME 2
00240222	C Edition	$49.99
00240227	B♭ Edition	$49.99
00240228	E♭ Edition	$49.99
00240229	Bass Clef Edition	$49.99
00240293	C Edition 6 x 9	$39.99
00125900	B♭ Edition 6 x 9	$39.99
00125900	The Real Book – Mini Edition	$39.99
00204126	Backing Tracks on USB Flash Drive	$55.00
00204131	C Edition – USB Flash Drive Pack	$85.00

VOLUME 3
00240233	C Edition	$49.99
00240284	B♭ Edition	$49.99
00240285	E♭ Edition	$49.99
00240286	Bass Clef Edition	$49.99
00240338	C Edition 6 x 9	$39.99

VOLUME 4
00240296	C Edition	$49.99
00103348	B♭ Edition	$49.99
00103349	E♭ Edition	$49.99
00103350	Bass Clef Edition	$49.99

VOLUME 5
00240349	C Edition	$49.99
00175278	B♭ Edition	$49.99
00175279	E♭ Edition	$49.99

VOLUME 6
00240534	C Edition	$49.99
00223637	E♭ Edition	$49.99

Also available:
00154230	The Real Bebop Book C Edition	$34.99
00295069	The Real Bebop Book E♭ Edition	$34.99
00295068	The Real Bebop Book B♭ Edition	$34.99
00240264	The Real Blues Book	$39.99
00310910	The Real Bluegrass Book	$39.99
00240223	The Real Broadway Book	$39.99
00240440	The Trane Book	$25.00
00125426	The Real Country Book	$45.00
00269721	The Real Miles Davis Book C Edition	$29.99
00269723	The Real Miles Davis Book B♭ Edition	$29.99
00240355	The Real Dixieland Book C Edition	$39.99
00294853	The Real Dixieland Book E♭ Edition	$39.99
00122335	The Real Dixieland Book B♭ Edition	$39.99
00240235	The Duke Ellington Real Book	$29.99
00240268	The Real Jazz Solos Book	$44.99
00240348	The Real Latin Book C Edition	$39.99
00127107	The Real Latin Book B♭ Edition	$39.99
00120809	The Pat Metheny Real Book C Edition	$34.99
00252119	The Pat Metheny Real Book B♭ Edition	$29.99
00240358	The Charlie Parker Real Book C Edition	$25.00
00275997	The Charlie Parker Real Book E♭ Edition	$25.00
00118324	The Real Pop Book C Edition – Vol. 1	$45.00
00295066	The Real Pop Book B♭ Edition – Vol. 1	$39.99
00286451	The Real Pop Book C Edition – Vol. 2	$45.00
00240331	The Bud Powell Real Book	$25.00
00240437	The Real R&B Book C Edition	$45.00
00276590	The Real R&B Book B♭ Edition	$45.00
00240313	The Real Rock Book	$39.99
00240323	The Real Rock Book – Vol. 2	$39.99
00240359	The Real Tab Book	$39.99
00240317	The Real Worship Book	$35.00

THE REAL CHRISTMAS BOOK
00240306	C Edition	$39.99
00240345	B♭ Edition	$35.00
00240346	E♭ Edition	$35.00
00240347	Bass Clef Edition	$35.00

THE REAL VOCAL BOOK
00240230	Volume 1 High Voice	$40.00
00240307	Volume 1 Low Voice	$40.00
00240231	Volume 2 High Voice	$39.99
00240308	Volume 2 Low Voice	$39.99
00240391	Volume 3 High Voice	$39.99
00240392	Volume 3 Low Voice	$39.99
00118318	Volume 4 High Voice	$39.99
00118319	Volume 4 Low Voice	$39.99

Complete song lists online at www.halleonard.com